Hispanic Heritage

Hispanic Heritage

Title List

Cuban Americans

Exiles from an Island Home

by Autumn Libal

Mason Crest Publishers

Philadelphia

Mason Crest Publishers Inc.

370 Reed Road

Broomall, Pennsylvania 19008

(866) MCP-BOOK (toll free)

First printing

1 2 3 4 5 6 7 8 9 10

Library of Congress Cataloging-in-Publication Data

Libal, Autumn.

  Cuban Americans : exiles from an island home / by Autumn Libal.

    p. cm. —— (Hispanic heritage)

  Includes index.

  Audience: Grades 9-12.

  ISBN 1-59084-928-0   ISBN 1-59084-924-8 (series)

  1. Cuban Americans—Juvenile literature. 2. Immigrants—United States—Juvenile literature. 3. Exiles—United States—Juvenile literature. I. Title. II. Hispanic heritage (Philadelphia, Pa.)

  E184.C97L53 2005

  973'.04687291——dc22

2004014998

Interior design by Dianne Hodack.

Produced by Harding House Publishing Service, Inc., Vestal, NY.

Cover design by Dianne Hodack.

Printed and bound in the Hashemite Kingdom of Jordan.

Contents

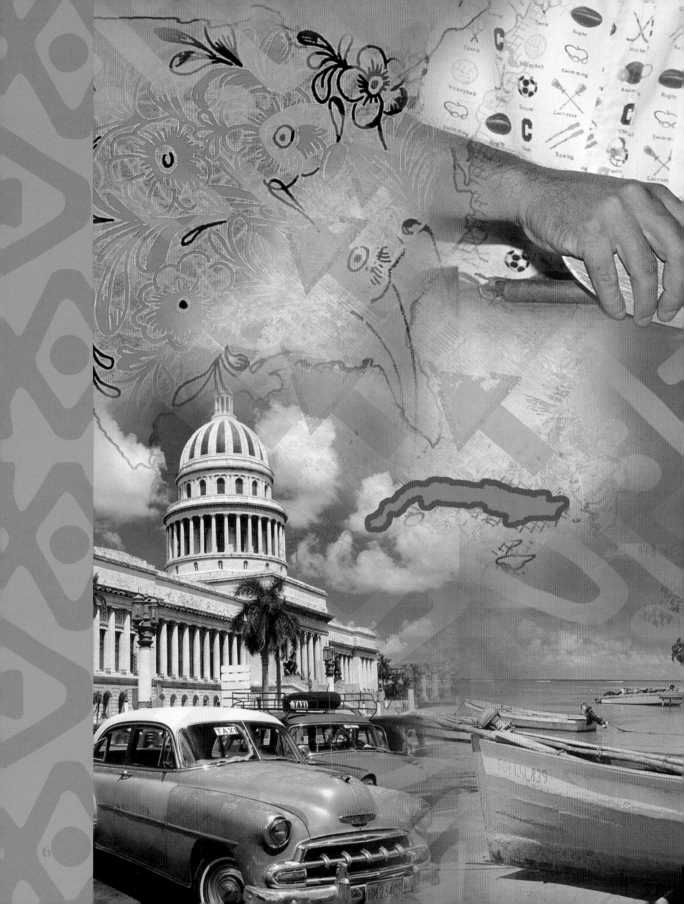

Introduction

by José E. Limón, Ph.D.

ven before there was a United States, Hispanics were present in what would become this country. Beginning in the sixteenth century, Spanish explorers traversed North America, and their explorations encouraged settlement as early as the sixteenth century in what is now northern New Mexico and Florida, and as late as the mid-eighteenth century in what is now southern Texas and California.

Later, in the nineteenth century, following Spain's gradual withdrawal from the New World, Mexico in particular established its own distinctive presence in what is now the southwestern part of the United States, a presence reinforced in the first half of the twentieth century by substantial immigration from that country. At the close of the nineteenth century, the U.S. war with Spain brought Cuba and Puerto Rico into an interactive relationship with the United States, the latter in a special political and economic affiliation with the United States even as American power influenced the course of almost every other Latin American country.

The books in this series remind us of these historical origins, even as each explores the present reality of different Hispanic groups. Some of these books explore the contemporary social origins—what social scientists call the "push" factors—behind the accelerating Hispanic immigration to America: political instability, economic underdevelopment and crisis, environmental degradation, impoverished or wholly absent educational systems, and other circumstances contribute to many Latin Americans deciding they will be better off in the United States.

And, for the most part, they will be. The vast majority come to work and work very hard, in order to earn better wages than they would back home. They fill significant labor needs in the U.S. economy and contribute to the economy through lower consumer prices and sales taxes.

When they leave their home countries, many immigrants may initially fear that they are leaving behind vital and important aspects of their home cultures: the Spanish language, kinship ties, food, music, folklore, and the arts. But as these books also make clear, culture is a fluid thing, and these native cultures are not only brought to America, they are also replenished in the United States in fascinating and novel ways. These books further suggest to us that Hispanic groups enhance American culture as a whole.

Our country—especially the young, future leaders who will read these books—can only benefit by the fair and full knowledge these authors provide about the socio-historical origins and contemporary cultural manifestations of America's Hispanic heritage.

Luis Rodríguez, Los Chaparros, *1997*

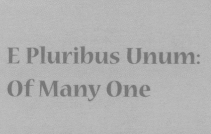

E Pluribus Unum:
Of Many One

If you were asked to describe a typical American, what do you think you would say? What would your typical American look like? What clothing would he or she wear? What language would he speak? What music would she like? Where would he be from? What job would she have? Hopefully you would soon see that it's impossible to describe a typical American, because Americans come from all different backgrounds and have diverse ways of life.

Artwork
Each chapter features the work of Cuban artist Louis Rodrigues. His bright colors, whimsical style, and lively compositions represent the heart of Cuban culture.

Children in the Cuban community

Cuban Americans may not immediately come to mind when you think of your "typical" American, but they have a significant population in the United States. There are approximately 1.38 million Cuban Americans in the United States today. That's just a little less than the population of North and South Dakota combined! In fact, approximately one in every 210 Americans is of Cuban descent. In this book, we will explore the Cuban American experience throughout history and in the present day. Along the way, we will see that Cuban Americans have become an important part of the United States' cultural *milieu*.

E Pluribus Unum

milieu: environment or social surroundings.

immigrants: people who come from one place and settle in another.

oppressed: kept in subservience.

exploited: taken advantage of.

diversity: the condition of being different, varied.

The United States is made up of many cultural groups. The national motto on the Great Seal of the United States reads, E Pluribus Unum, which means Of Many One. This motto originally referred to the thirteen original colonies that joined together to make one nation. Today we recognize that E Pluribus Unum is an apt description of America as a nation of *immigrants*, a nation where people from countries and cultures all over the world have joined together to make something new and unique. Sometimes different groups within the United States have clashed violently, and frequently throughout American history certain groups have *oppressed* and *exploited* others. Today, however, more and more Americans are realizing that each cultural group makes valuable contributions to America, and *diversity* is one of the greatest gifts the United States can offer to the world.

Cultural Glue

The term Cuban American describes a specific cultural group of people in the United States—but what exactly is culture? You could say it's a set of characteristics—like customs, behaviors, artistic expression, and beliefs—that are shared by a certain group. Or you might think of culture as a glue that binds people together into a community. Things like *nationality*, region, religion, age, or even occupation can act as cultural "glue," adhering together people who share common traits. That's why Cubans, West-Coast Americans, Hindus, teens, business people, theatergoers—any group that is brought together by shared characteristics—could be defined as a culture.

At the same time, however, cultures do not have clear divisions. Cultures influence each other, adapt, evolve, and commingle—their glue seeps out and mixes with other cultural glues. Music from one part of the world influences music across the globe. Clothing styles popular among one group of people spread to other groups. Words from one language are adopted into many other languages. This mixing of cultural glues causes people to bond in interesting and sometimes unexpected ways, and one person might become a member of numerous cultures. Perhaps nowhere in the world is this truer than in the United States of America.

Each tile in a mosaic retains its unique identity, just as cultural groups within the United States have their own characteristics and values.

A Human Mosaic

plurality of cultures is one of the things that makes the United States vibrant with the potential to be one of the most tolerant, humane, productive, and innovative places in the world. Many people describe the United States as a melting pot—a place where lots of people mix and *amalgamate* into one American soup. The melting-pot analogy implies that in America, cultural groups lose their individual identities as they are broken down and absorbed into a new American *alloy*.

For many people in America, however, the melting-pot analogy is not applicable. Most

integrity: wholeness; completeness; uncorrupted condition.

Americans, whether they have lived in the United States for generations or have newly immigrated to the country, do not want to lose their cultural identities. They may want to live in America and even be "American," but they don't want to be melted down in a culture-dissolving pot. A better analogy for North America would be a mosaic. A mosaic is a picture made of many individual tiles glued together. When viewed from a distance, the lines between the tiles blur, and the mosaic looks like one big picture. When examined up close, each individual tile can be identified for its singularity, particular characteristics, and beauty, and it becomes clear that the mosaic is not one picture at all but a collection of independent elements. Sometimes, as people adapt to life in America, it may seem on the surface that they have lost their cultural traits. If we look a little closer, however, we see that people's cultures infuse and affect even the most "American" things they do.

Cultural Identity

evertheless, living among a diversity of cultures can present unique challenges for a society's members. Maintaining their cultural *integrity* when barraged by other cultures' practices and beliefs is perhaps the biggest challenge facing cultural groups in the United States. When glue gets old, it dries out, crumbles, and loses its ability to stick. Cultural "glue" is similar; it needs to be refreshed or renewed on a regular basis if it is going to continue to hold people together. Participating in one's cultural community (for example by doing things like visiting

Cuban Americans are part of a larger linguistic, or language, group called Hispanic—people who speak Spanish or have Spanish ancestry but are not from Spain. The Spanish language and Hispanic cultures are important parts of North American culture. Hispanic people are now the United States' largest minority. Spanish appears on everything from street signs to nutrition labels. English has adopted thousands of Spanish words like cafeteria, mustang, patio, and mosquito. Hispanic foods are enjoyed in millions of North American homes, and Hispanic artists, actors, musicians, athletes, activists, and other individuals enrich all Americans' lives.

Most people of Spanish-speaking heritage, however, prefer to not be thought of simply as Hispanic. They would rather be identified by their individual cultural group—as Mexican, Puerto Rican, Cuban, or Chilean, for example—than lumped together into a melting-pot term like Hispanic.

Music is one force that unites a cultural community.

with members of your culture, talking about your beliefs, participating in your traditions, attending your cultural festivals, speaking your language, or teaching others about your culture) is a process of renewal that keeps cultural glue fresh and moist. After a number of generations living in America away from their larger cultural community, a people's cultural glue could begin to dry and crack. The cultural glue from their surroundings may seep in, and eventually, the people could feel more connected to American culture than to their original culture. Although it can be a great struggle to resist *acculturation* and *assimilation*, by participating in regular cultural renewal, many groups succeed in maintaining their individual cultures, even over many generations.

acculturation: the process of adopting another culture.

assimilation: absorption into a larger body.

economics: the theory and practice of wealth production and distribution.

Cuban Americans

Cuban Americans have been remarkably successful in maintaining their cultural identity in the United States. The Cuban population in the United States is made up of both Cubans (people who were born and raised in Cuba) and Cuban Americans (people of Cuban descent who were born or raised in the United States or have taken American citizenship). As you will soon see, Cubans and Cuban Americans have contributed greatly to today's America. At the same time, they retain strong connections to their island home, maintain pride and participation in their culture, and remain intimately involved in Cuban politics and *economics*. In fact, Cubans as a group keep closer ties to their homeland than any other immigrant group in America.

he countries of Central and South America and the Caribbean are often collectively called Latin America. Many Latin American people living in the United States and Canada today prefer the term Latino to Hispanic. The term Latino incorporates Latin American people from multiple backgrounds rather than separating out people of Spanish descent. Many Spanish-speaking people have non-Spanish ancestors. Furthermore, though Spanish is spoken by a majority of people in Latin America, other languages are also spoken. For example, Portuguese is the official language of Brazil, and French is the official language of French-Guiana. These Portuguese and French speakers are not considered Hispanic, but they are considered Latino.

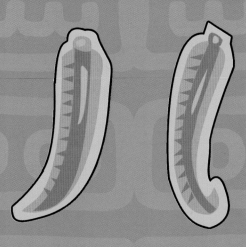

Cuban restaurants preserve one aspect of Cuban culture in the United States.

Students playing traditional Cuban music

This is partly because of Cuba's close proximity to the United States, but mostly it is because a large portion of Cubans in the United States never intended to make this their permanent home. Circumstances may have forced them to America's shores, but they believed that one day they would return home to Cuba.

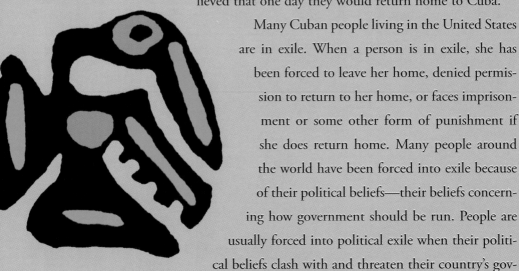

Many Cuban people living in the United States are in exile. When a person is in exile, she has been forced to leave her home, denied permission to return to her home, or faces imprisonment or some other form of punishment if she does return home. Many people around the world have been forced into exile because of their political beliefs—their beliefs concerning how government should be run. People are usually forced into political exile when their political beliefs clash with and threaten their country's government or most powerful individuals. When most people

The island of Cuba

think of Cubans' exile in America, they think of Fidel Castro (Cuba's current president) and his *socialist* government. Cuba, however, has a turbulent history, and political exiles have been coming from Cuba to America for at least two hundred years. Understanding this history is necessary to understanding Cuban Americans' lives today.

socialist: one who believes that wealth and the means for producing it should be community owned rather than privately owned.

Habla Español

cultura (cool-too-rah): culture

exiliado (akes-eel-e-ah-do): exile (a person)

exilio (akes-eel-ee-oh): exile (the condition)

Luis Rodríguez, Camino a Cristo, *1997*

2

An Island Home:
From Spanish Conquest
to American Domination

The canoes ran aground, pebbles rolling and crunching beneath their weight. Four hundred pairs of feet swung over the sides and into the waves. The waters churned as the travelers splashed toward the island. They had survived the ocean journey, but could they survive what was ahead? Pulling the canoes ashore, the people knew this island would be their final refuge—or it would be their grave.

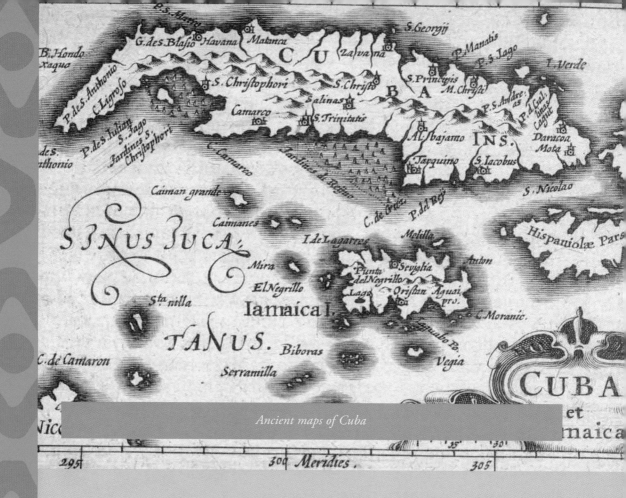

Ancient maps of Cuba

The travelers' leader, Hatuey, strode purposefully up the sandy beach. The island's inhabitants ran forward, arms spread in welcome. *They have no idea,* Hatuey thought sadly, *of what is awaiting them. They cannot imagine the story I have to tell.*

Hatuey's tale was a horrific one indeed. He told of light-skinned men who wore impenetrable armor and carried weapons that were harder than stone, who thought nothing of beheading a child for sport, who ordered dogs to tear open other men's stomachs, and who chopped off the hands and feet of Hatuey's people and left them in the bloody dirt to die. They were men, he said, who treated other human beings worse than they treated animals. They would come to this island, Hatuey warned, preaching about a forgiving (and white-skinned) god. They would say that all they did was for the glory of this god. But really, Hatuey proclaimed, their god was gold, and all their horrific deeds were part of a crazy lust for the yellow metal. Hatuey urged the island's people to join him and flee into the mountains. From there, he said, they could attack these horrible men when they

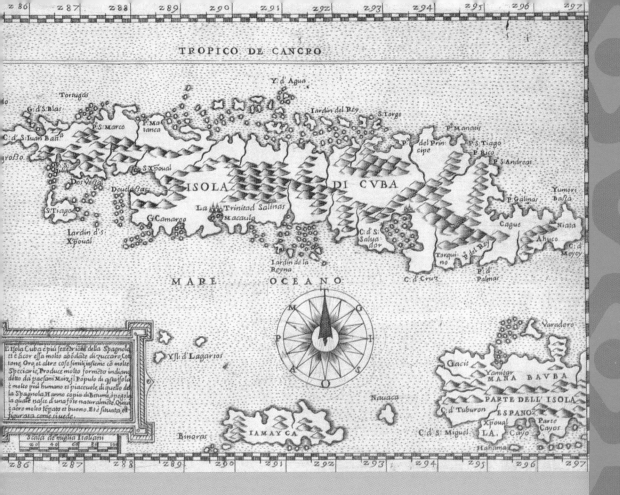

came and drive them from the island before it was destroyed as Hatuey's own home had been.

The island's inhabitants listened to Hatuey's tale, but few could believe it was true. Yes, they knew of these light-skinned men; a few had already visited the island and even seized some of the island's people. But how could any human behave as Hatuey described? Hatuey's people marched into the mountains, but few of the island's inhabitants followed.

Hatuey, however, was right. The men did come with their armor, swords, dogs, and god. The atrocities began, and from their hideaways in the mountains, Hatuey's people fought. It was the island's first revolution, but the revolution failed. Hatuey was captured and sentenced to be burned at the stake. Just before his death, Hatuey's executioners offered him a chance for redemption. If he were to accept their god and agree to be *baptized*, the executioners explained, he would go to heaven to live with their god in everlasting peace. Hatuey thought about the proposition and then asked one question: did these light-skinned men go to heaven as well? The executioners assured him that yes, any good Christian goes to heaven. Hatuey made his decision. If these horrific men were to be found in heaven, then he wished to have no part of it. The fire was lit, and Hatuey became a *martyr* for his people.

The Meeting of Two Cultures

atuey's legendary struggle and death occurred on an island called Cuba. It is the largest island in an archipelago, or group of islands, that makes up the Republic of Cuba. Cuba is located about ninety miles (approximately 150 kilometers) south of Florida and has an area of approximately 43,000 square miles (111,000 square kilometers), making it slightly smaller than the state of Pennsylvania.

Like much of the Americas, the main language spoken today in Cuba is Spanish. This, however, does not mean that Cuban people are Spanish, for they do not come from Spain and they have a culture that is quite distinct from Spanish culture. To call all Spanish-speaking people in the Americas Spanish would make no more sense than to call all English-speaking people in the Americas English. But if the people of Cuba are not Spanish, how did Spanish become the main language of the island?

In 1492, a world-changing event occurred. Christopher

Christopher Columbus

An early portrayal of the Arawak

Columbus, an Italian-born explorer working for the Spanish crown, landed on shores previously unknown to the *Western* world. This tale of Europeans' arrival in the Americas is often told with pride, as a romantic triumph of the human spirit of discovery. The truth, however, is that there was nothing romantic, grand, or triumphant about Columbus's arrival on these islands. Europeans' arrival in the Americas was characterized by grotesque greed and gruesome murder.

Columbus believed he had traveled full circle around the world and landed in the Indies, a part of Asia. Really, however, he had landed in the Bahamas in the Caribbean Sea. He explored a number of the islands, seized some of the people he encountered, and returned to Spain with lavish tales of a land heavy with gold, perfumed with spices, and teeming with people who would make perfect slaves.

Columbus returned to the Caribbean, and many Spaniards followed. Here, they found peaceful *Arawak* peoples living in the hundreds of thousands (perhaps even in the millions), who offered food, friendship, guidance, and their possessions. Columbus, his men, and those who followed, enslaved, tortured, and murdered these people. In just two years, hundreds of thousands of the native people had been killed at the hands of their tyrannical overlords, by the foreign diseases the Spanish carried, or by suicide—their only escape from the invaders. Within fifty years, only a few hundred of these people remained. In 150 years, perhaps every single Arawak was dead.

In 1511, less than twenty years after Columbus's first arrival, the legendary Hatuey gathered his remaining people and fled the island of Hispañola (the first island occupied by the Spanish) for neighboring Cuba. What happened on Hispañola, however, was repeated throughout the Americas, as first the Spanish and then other European powers such as the

Western: of or relating to Europe (and later North America).

Arawak: the Native peoples of the Carribean and northern and western South America. The Arawak tribes of Cuba were the Ciboney and the Tainos.

The landing of Columbus

29

colonial: relating to a period of time characterized by the seizing of colonies and eploitation of their people by other countries.

Portuguese, Dutch, French, and British seized these hitherto unknown lands.

In Cuba, as in the rest of the Caribbean, the Spanish hoped to find vast amounts of gold to finance their *colonial* aspirations. They soon learned that Columbus's reports were greatly exaggerated, and the island's gold was quickly depleted. To make money off the newly colonized land, they sold thousands of the Arawak as slaves, but with the Arawak quickly dying the slave trade would not hold out for long. Nevertheless, Cuba became extremely important to Spain. Its location within 150 miles (240 kilometers) of both Florida and Mexico made it a key part of Spain's trade routes and the perfect launching pad for colonial expeditions further into the Americas.

Slavery

oon the Spanish realized a new way Cuba could make them rich. The island's original inhabitants had grown manioc (a root vegetable), corn, potatoes, cotton, and tobacco—all crops that were foreign to the Spanish—to feed and support themselves. As the settlers exterminated the Native population, they seized the fertile farmland and learned to cultivate the native crops. But the Spanish also discovered that another crop would grow well in Cuba: sugarcane. They imported the cane (sugarcane originally came from Asia), and huge plantations arose. Sugar was Cuba's new gold, and thousands of workers were needed to tend the massive crops. Just as they had once

he European seizure of lands and enslavement of people that took place in the Americas occurred all over the globe. This period, in which European powers rushed to stake their claims over the world's land, people, and resources, was known as the colonial era. During the colonial era, European nations invaded every continent, enslaved millions of people, and extracted the countries' natural resources. Development in colonies was designed to benefit the colonizers while keeping the colonized people oppressed. The native governments were crushed, and all wealth generated by the colonies' resources went to foreign hands rather than for the benefit of the Native people.

An example of the Spanish art style in Cuba

enslaved the Arawak peoples and kidnapped them to sell in Europe, now the Spanish enslaved African peoples and kidnapped them to work Cuba's plantations.

Within three hundred years of Columbus's arrival, a new Cuban population had replaced the original Arawak peoples. Four main groups made up this deeply *stratified* society: Spanish, criollos, African, and mulatto. The Spanish held the most powerful positions in Cuba, namely state, church, and military positions. Many came to the Americas hoping to make a name for themselves in the colonies and then move up to more important positions back in Europe. The criollos were people of Spanish descent who were Cuban born. Whereas the Spanish controlled the political and military power, the criollos, who were mostly farmers and merchants, controlled much of Cuba's wealth. Now, too, there were the African slaves, and some of the African, Spanish, and criollos mixed. Cuban people of mixed heritage were called mulattos, a rather unkind term as it comes from the Spanish word for mule. Cuban people of African, criollo, and mulatto descent resented the Spaniards' authority and continued control over the island.

Cuban America

uring the colonial era, Spain not only aquired Caribbean and South and Central American lands, they also seized control of what is today the southern and western United

annexed: incorporated
into a larger body or
organization.

States. From the early years of Spanish domination, people moved throughout the Spanish empire, including between Cuba and North America. In fact, there were probably Cuban "Americans" long before there was even a United States of America. Even after the United States seized control over all of mainland North America, this movement continued. By the mid-1800s, Cubans were coming to America for vacations, study, and business. Likewise, thousands of Americans not only visited Cuba, but moved to Cuba to work and start their own businesses. Discontent and revolutions on the island, however, would eventually send most of these Americans, as well as large numbers of Cubans, north.

Hatuey had launched the first Cuban revolution in the 1500s and failed. By the mid-1800s, Cuba's population again wanted freedom from its colonial overlord. In fact, all over the Americas, colonies were rebelling against the European yoke. Wars for independence had already been fought and won by both the United States and Mexico. Cubans, however, were divided over what independence from Spain should mean. Some Cubans, especially free blacks, slaves, and mulattos, thought Cuba should become completely independent. Many criollos, whose farms depended on slave labor and who feared an uprising of Cuba's black population, wanted to remain part of Spain for the protection its military forces could provide. Others, again mostly well-to-do criollos, wanted Cuba to be *annexed* to the United States, who was now Cuba's largest trading partner.

any Spanish-speaking countries in the Americas today have large and even majority mestizo (people of mixed Spanish and Native ancestry) populations. In Cuba, however, the Native population was decimated so completely and replaced so quickly by African slaves that few mestizo populations developed or endured. Although most scholars believe Cuba's indigenous population was completely eradicated, there is a small population of Cubans who believe they are descended from survivors of the original tribes.

Throughout the 1800s, Cubans who advocated for independence from Spain found themselves exiled, often to the United States. These exiles played a large role in shaping both Cuban and U.S. opinion toward the issue of the island's independence. As early as the 1820s, political newspapers devoted to the Cuba question were being published in New York City and smuggled to Cuba and other Cubans abroad. In fact, by 1850, New York City had become an important hub of the Cuban independence movement. There were only about one thousand Cubans in the United States, but many of these were vocal members of intellectual and political circles.

According to James S. Olson and Judith E. Olson, authors of *Cuban Americans: From Trauma to Triumph*, between the 1840s and 1850s, leadership of the Cuban exile community was concentrated in New York. These highly political and intellectual leaders favored the annexation of Cuba to the United States. Although they thought Cuba should break from Spain, they believed this transfer of power should be accomplished through peaceful, diplomatic means, and that the powerful United States would be best equipped to handle such negotiations.

In the 1850s, leadership of the exile community shifted to a more *radical* group based in New Orleans. This group rejected diplomacy (after years of unsuccessful attempts, they concluded there was no diplomatic solution to Spain's continued control of Cuba) and the idea of annexation to the United States. Although joining the United States might be a possibility to consider in the future, they believed that first Cuba needed to mount an armed *insurrection* from within its own borders. According to this school of thought, people outside Cuba were not going to be able to negotiate Cuba's independence from Spain; Cubans on the island were going to have to fight for that independence themselves. In the late 1860s, the leaders of this movement also did something none of the Cuban *nationalist* movements had done before: they denounced slavery and said it should be abolished immediately.

The sugar plantations in Cuba still relied on slave labor, and Spain, though reforming

Carlos Manuel de Céspedes

General Maceo

some slavery laws, refused to completely abolish slavery in its colonies. The *expatriates* knew they couldn't kick Spain out of Cuba themselves. They needed the island's population to heed their cry and take up arms. By denouncing slavery, they gained the support of the island's slaves, free blacks, and many mulattos. For the first time since Hatuey's sixteenth-century struggle, Cuba's citizens were finally ready to revolt.

The Ten Years War

he first battles in the new Cuban revolution began in 1868. Carlos Manuel de Céspedes, a member of the wealthy class, was fed up with Spain's continued rule. He freed his slaves, enlisted many of them as his army, and launched his first attacks. Meeting with some initial military success and popular support, Céspedes formed a government and declared Cuba independent. He was now Cuba's first president, but neither Spain nor Cubans who supported Spain recognized his government. In a few years, Céspedes was *deposed*, and the struggle for independence continued; two very important military leaders emerged: Máximo Gómez and Antonio Maceo. Although the Cuban rebels were vastly outnumbered and outgunned, Gómez and Maceo resisted the Spanish forces and kept Cuba's hopes for independence alive.

Many Cubans, Cuban Americans, and American *abolitionists* saw Cuba's fight with Spain as a continuation of the fight against slavery and the struggle for freedom and equality. Some

radical: extreme views or beliefs.

insurrection: uprising; rebellion.

nationalist: patriotic; supporting a nation or national movement.

expatriates: people who have left their country for another.

deposed: removed from position.

abolitionists: people who wanted slavery abolished (destroyed).

resident Lincoln abolished slavery in 1863, and the outcome of the U.S. Civil War 1861–1865) made President Lincoln's decision binding on the whole country.

José Martí

Americans—both of Cuban and non-Cuban descent—even supported the Cuban cause by smuggling weapons and money to the island's revolutionaries. Supporters also pressured the American government to back the rebellion.

The U.S. government watched with interest as events in Cuba unfolded, but remained reluctant to get involved. Meanwhile, the revolutionaries' struggle wore on. Then in 1878, ten years after the rebellion began, the revolutionary government signed a treaty with Spain that brought an official end to the war without achieving Cuban freedom. Maceo, Gómez, and other important military leaders refused to accept this insult and left Cuba, hoping to rebuild their forces abroad. Approximately five thousand Cuban exiles now lived in the United States, and many others lived elsewhere in the Caribbean, Central America, and South America.

Maceo, Gómez, and other exiles spent the next eight years trying to reignite the revolution. In 1886, however, Spain finally abolished slavery in Cuba. *Appeased* by the decision, Gomez declared an end to the revolutionary movement. Spain may have believed that Cuba was theirs again, but by the early 1890s, revolutionary embers rekindled.

José Martí and Independence

y 1895, Cuba and Puerto Rico were Spain's only remaining American colonies. But as Cubans dreamed of independence, another colonial power was lusting after their island. The European powers were losing their grip on colonies around the world, but the growing United States was taking on many characteristics of the colonial countries that had given birth to it. The United States had already seized huge amounts of land from the Native populations and from Mexico. It followed the Civil War with a wholesale slaughter of the Native American tribes and seizure of their lands. Now the United States had focused its eyes on Cuba.

Previous revolutionaries had favored annexation to the United States, Cuba's number-one trading partner. But a new revolutionary leader named José Martí completely rejected the idea. A Cuban exile living in New York, Martí was a poet, journalist, and gifted communicator who rallied Cubans to the rev-

appeased: calmed, brought to a peaceful end.

"The Cuban problem needs, rather than a political solution, a social solution, and... the latter cannot be achieved except through mutual love, and forgiveness between the races."

Letter from José Martí to Antonio Maceo, July 1882.

Sign found in Havana

39

n 1492, Columbus reported that the Caribbean Islands could give the king and queen of Spain fertile pastures, plentiful spices, "as much gold as they need . . . and as many slaves as they ask." By the 1890s, Americans sounded eerily reminiscent of Columbus. An 1891 article in the *Detroit Free Press* declared what many American businessmen and politicians believed when it stated, "Cuba would make one of the finest states in the Union, and if American wealth, enterprise and genius once invaded the superb island, it would become a veritable hive of industry in addition to being one of the most fertile gardens of the world. . . . We should act at once and make this possible."

olutionary cause with his passionate words. The movement's message now was freedom— freedom from slavery, freedom from Spain, and freedom from the United States. The revolutionaries knew that under U.S. domination, Cuba would continue to be oppressed and exploited as it was under Spain.

In 1895, Martí returned to Cuba with his revolutionary forces. He was killed in battle shortly after, but this time the rebel movement could not be *quelled*. Over time, José Martí rose to *iconic* status in Cuba. He continues to be celebrated as the father of Cuban independence.

For three years after Martí's death, fighting in Cuba mounted, and fear and outrage in the United States grew as well. Previously, the U.S. government had been reluctant to get involved in Cuba's fight with Spain. Now, however, more than seven thousand Americans lived in Cuba and ran profitable businesses there. American companies owned many of Cuba's sugar plantations. With so many American economic interests threatened, the cries for U.S. involvement were louder than ever. In 1898, the United States sent battleships to Cuba's harbors. After one of those battleships, the *Maine*, mysteriously exploded, the United States blamed Spain and declared war. The mystery of the *Maine* was never solved, and Spain was never proved at fault, but within four months, the Spanish-American War was over. Spain, which had been engaged in decades of struggle with Cuba, surrendered not to the island's revolutionaries, but to the United States.

American Domination

Although Cuba had finally won its independence from Spain, it still was not free. Now the United States marched its troops onto Cuban soil and demanded the central role in building Cuba's new government. The United States made a mockery of Cuba's new independence by introducing the Platt Amendment, which required U.S. intervention in any situation that might threaten the island's independence; it handed control of Cuba's trade and international affairs to America; and it allowed the United States to build a military base on Cuba's

quelled: overwhelmed.

iconic: symbolic; characteristic of or embodying a larger cultural ideal.

Statue of José Martí

Gerardo Machado

Guantánamo Bay. (Though the Platt Amendment was abolished in 1934, the U.S. military base remains.) In 1902, the United States claimed Cuba was finally an independent nation, but in reality Cuba did not have *sovereignty*.

Americans had been running businesses and purchasing property in Cuba for years, and now these American influences only increased. Cuban politicians became increasingly corrupt as they used American political and business connections for personal gain. By the early 1930s, Cuba's political situation was in crisis.

Gerardo Machado was the man in power. Called a president, he was really a *dictator*. Once installed in the presidency, Machado used bribery, military force, and even murder to control the government and annihilate his opponents. Many Cubans despised Machado, but the only ones who could safely speak out against him were the Cubans living abroad and therefore out of Machado's reach. Demonstrations held by Cubans living in the United States were important parts of the political movement to see Machado deposed. In 1933, the United States played a large role in orchestrating his overthrow and bringing a new leader, Fulgencio Batista, to power.

The Reign of Batista

t the beginning, Batista was a little-known sergeant in Cuba's military. After orchestrating the *coup d'etat* that forced Machado from power, Batista became Chief of the Military and the true "power behind the throne." He appointed a series of puppet presidents, who were Cuba's leaders in name only. In reality, they simply did Batista's bidding. At first, as he legalized *labor unions*, guaranteed a minimum wage, instituted job-creation programs, and improved some social services, it seemed that Batista would be good for Cuba. Batista, however, was deeply corrupt, and as time wore on, his corruption affected people at all levels of Cuban society.

In 1940, Cuba had its first free elections, and Batista was elected president (an outcome that was hardly surprising, considering that Batista, like Machado before him, was not above using violence, even murder, to do away with his opponents). His presidency, however, was short lived. In the next election, held in 1944, Batista was voted out of office. Under the guise

sovereignty: *complete and undisputed independence.*

dictator: *a person who rules with absolute power.*

coup d'etat: *a seizure of power, often through violent or military means.*

labor unions: *groups formed to protect the rights and interests of workers.*

y the time Machado came to power, about 34,000 Cubans lived in the United States. The vast majority of Cubans settled in south Florida, which was still close to Cuba and had a climate and landscape similar to the island's. The Cubans who settled in south Florida brought an important art form with them that became a major industry in the state: cigar rolling. Cubans have long been known for making the best cigars in the world, and it takes years to learn the techniques to roll one of these fine cigars. As Florida's cigar industry grew, many Cubans came to Florida to work. In the first half of the twentieth century, the Cuban American population may have been about 34,000, but tens of thousands more migrated to the United States for work and then returned to Cuba. The cigar industry was an extremely important part of the Florida economy. It also became an important source of funds to fuel Cuba's revolutionary movements.

of respecting the Cuban peoples' vote, Batista retired to Florida, but his reign was far from over. He spent the rest of the decade assembling his supporters and planning a return to power.

By 1952, Batista was back in Cuba and again running for the Cuban presidency. When it became apparent, however, that he could not win the election, he staged his second coup, overthrew the elected president, and declared himself Cuba's ruler. The United States, under President Dwight D. Eisenhower, recognized Batista and his government as *legitimate* a few weeks later.

Organized crime loved Batista. Under his new regime, Cuba's capital, Havana became known as "Latin Las Vegas" and "America's Playground." Huge casinos and hotels sprang up, built largely with government money. Batista personally took a cut of all gambling profits. Under Batista, the rich were getting richer, and the poor were getting poorer. The crime rate exploded, stirring deep unrest, but anyone who spoke out against Batista was in danger. He built a powerful military-police force, which seemed to focus less on punishing legitimate crimes than brutalizing the population and squelching all anti-government (and many far more *innocuous*) activities. Torture and murder were standard parts of the police force's frightening *repertoire*.

Thousands of Cubans were fleeing to America's shores every year. Through all the decades of revolution and political upheaval, however, few who left Cuba intended to make a permanent home in the United States. Cuban *refugees* and exiles in the United States kept faith that a truly democratic government would emerge, the danger would pass, and they would be able to return home.

legitimate: *lawful; sanctioned; recognized.*

innocuous: *harmless; causing no injury or offense.*

repertoire: *a stock or collection of regularly used techniques.*

refugees: *persons taking refuge from danger, usually in a foreign country.*

Cuban cabarets thrived under Batista.

🔳abla 🔳spañol

independencia (een-day-pane-dane-see-ah): independence

revolución (ray-voh-loo-see-own): revolution

libertad (lee-bare-tod): freedom

45

Luis Rodríguez, Ladrones de Gallinas, *1997*

3

A New Revolution and International Crisis

Che watched as his parents mulled over the small stack of household items. Every now and then they placed something in the open suitcase, but mostly they tossed their possessions aside to be distributed among family and neighbors. Che was only six years old, but he knew this wasn't the way things were supposed to be. Just a short time ago, his parents had supported the great revolutionary movement led by Fidel Castro. In fact, Che had been named after one of the revolutionaries. His father had told him how when the new government came to power, the whole country had been flush with hope. But now, like many others, his family was taking flight. Che wondered how his life had turned so quickly upside down, and what life in this new place—America—would be like.

Che Guevara's image on a Cuban building

Castro's Revolution

n the 1950s, Cubans in America thought the day of their homecoming might be drawing near. While Batista, corruption, and crime rings reigned, there could be no democracy in Cuba, and in 1953 a new leader, Fidel Castro, was fanning revolutionary flames. Castro was a young, well-educated lawyer from a wealthy family. Some say Castro had an insatiable appetite for power. Others say he was willing to sacrifice everything for the cause of Cuban freedom. What is undisputed is that Castro, like José Martí before him, was a gifted speaker who stirred people's hearts and imaginations with his words. He *invoked* Martí's name often and urged Cubans to return to their hero's ideals.

By July 1953, Castro had assembled a small group of revolutionaries—only 111 men and two women in all. On the twenty-sixth of that month, this ill-equipped force made its first stand against Batista by attacking a military *garrison* of one thousand soldiers.

Castro's first attack became known as the 26th of July Movement for its spirit rather than for its military success. Although only three rebels were killed in the initial attack, eighty were captured, and most of these were tortured and then executed. Within days, Castro too was found, but his life was saved by a merciful military commander. He and the other survivors were imprisoned, but none were about to give up the cause.

Although militarily unsuccessful, the attack brought new life and purpose to the anti-Batista movement. By 1954, Batista was reelected; feeling confident in his reign, he *pardoned* Castro and the remaining imprisoned rebels. Shortly after their release, the rebels followed Castro to Mexico. There they rebuilt the 26th of July Movement.

Cuban expatriates once again played an important role in the revolutionary movement. Castro toured the U.S. Cuban communities raising money for the cause, and his forces used these funds to purchase weapons and supplies to survive during their grueling training in *guerrilla* warfare. They were joined by non-Cuban revolutionaries who were willing to give their lives for Cuban freedom, the most notable being Ernesto "Che" Guevara—an Argentine doctor who would become one of

invoked: called on.

garrison: a military installation.

pardoned: excused for a crime and released from its consequences.

guerrilla: irregular warfare, characterized by being unconventional, radical, or aggressive.

Older Cubans still remember Batista's corruption.

Latin America's most famous revolutionaries. While this rebel band hiked, climbed mountains, ran drills, learned to make explosives, and studied the writings of José Martí, discontent in Cuba grew. Finally, eighteen months after coming to Mexico, Castro decided it was time for his forces to make a glorious return to Cuba.

On November 25, 1956, Castro and his followers hastily boarded the *Granma*, a retired leisure-yacht-turned-revolutionary vessel. They held their breath as they slipped out of the Mexican harbor, avoiding the city lights that danced across the water. Once safely away from shore, the men wondered if the sun-bleached, ocean-battered, and now horribly overloaded *Granma* could even survive the 150-mile (240-kilometer) crossing to Cuba's shores.

By the time the rebels arrived on December 2, things didn't look good. The rebels had

Havana, Cuba

made poor time, and Batista's forces had already been alerted. Celia Sanchez, one of the women who had fought with Castro on July 26, 1953, was waiting with trucks and supplies at the designated landing sight. But when a military plane roared overhead, the rebels knew they had been spotted. Fearful of what awaited them on shore, they changed course, landing the *Granma* miles from Sanchez's position. Forced to wade through the swamp to reach land, the rebels left most of their supplies and weapons behind. Exhausted from the journey, carrying few

weapons, having no food, and feeling Batista's forces closing in, the rebels were now extremely vulnerable. In the distance, the Sierra Maestra Mountains rose in a majestic tangle of jungle and clouds. Castro knew if they could reach the mountains, they would be safe.

Only a handful of the eighty-two people who departed the *Granma* reached those mountains. Three days into the journey, they were ambushed. Batista's forces showed no mercy; they even killed those trying to surrender. The remaining forces scattered and fled.

Sign commemorating the twentieth anniversary of Granma

Over the next two weeks, many more were captured or killed, and by the time they regrouped in the mountains, only twelve remained.

Once again, Castro's revolutionary movement seemed close to failure, but Castro declared to his remaining force, "The days of the dictatorship are numbered!" Safe within the impenetrable mountains and buoyed by their leader's faith, the revolutionaries again rebuilt their ranks.

Within weeks, the rebels were raiding military installations. Word of their successes leaked past the media censors, and steady streams of recruits flowed in. Within a year, the ranks had swelled to three hundred and counting. An elaborate checkpoint and telephone system was laid, an armory and hospital were established, and a broadcasting system, *Radio Rebelde*, transmitted their message across Cuba. The rebels also earned the respect and support of the local peasants.

Fidel Castro was popular with ordinary people.

The peasants were able to use the rebels' hospital, were given *literacy* education by the rebel forces, and enjoyed wage increases after the rebels gave an ultimatum to sugar-mill owners: increase wages or see your mills burn. The peasants repaid the rebels' kindness by planting crops to feed the forces and clearing roads for their vehicles. Both at home and abroad, Castro's reputation as a man of the people grew, and so did his support.

Determined to squelch the uprising once and for all, in May 1958, Batista sent ten thousand soldiers marching into the mountain stronghold. Just a few hundred men against an army of ten thousand; the odds could hardly have been worse. Yet the rebels, with their knowledge of the mountains and their elaborate support systems, seemed unconquerable. The military soon had little will to fight the now-popular movement.

By August, the army was in retreat. Castro's forces emerged from the mountains and seized control of the province. On January 1, 1959, Batista and his closest supporters boarded a plane under the cover of darkness and fled to the Dominican Republic. The next day, the rebel army began a six-day, 500-mile victory parade from the southern city of Santiago to Havana in the north. Cuba's citizenry lined up along the entire length of the route to cheer their new leader.

literacy: reading and writing.

reprisal: retaliation; vengeful punishment.

International Crisis and a Great Migration

he day Batista took flight marked the beginning of an unprecedented flood of Cubans from their homeland. Most in Cuba were jubilant at the tyrant's downfall, but Batista's supporters, some of whom had grown rich from his corrupt policies or performed "dirty-work" for the fallen leader, feared *reprisal* from the new government. While Cubans who had fled Batista considered returning to the island, those who supported Batista were now on the run, many coming to American shores. Later, as Castro's new government put members of Batista's military and police forces on trial for crimes against the Cuban people, and many of those convicted were sentenced to death, even more Cubans decided to journey abroad.

For the most part, however, the Cuban population was dizzy with joy and pride in their new leader. When those accused and convicted of crimes under Batista's regime were sentenced to death by firing squad, it seemed like justice. When Castro spoke of reforming the government, economy, and society to establish true equality, it too seemed like justice. When Castro declared there would be a new peaceful and love-filled Cuba, it seemed

Castro attending a celebration with school children

53

prophetic. Castro was the warrior for the underdog. He had already displayed his overwhelming concern for Cuba's poverty-stricken masses by his actions in the Sierra Maestra Mountains. No Cuban leader had ever thought Cuba's most numerous and needy were important before, and now Castro was their hero.

While most of Cuba's citizenry rallied behind their new leader, American politicians and businesses held their breath. Richard Nixon, then vice president of the United States, echoed many people's feelings when he stated that Castro was, at best, very *naïve*, and at worst (and what Nixon was convinced was the case) a *communist*.

During the 1950s, practically no insult could be worse than to be labeled a communist. Engaged in the *Cold War* with the Soviet Union, America was in an anti-communist frenzy. People suspected of communist sympathies lost their jobs and were even jailed. Any form of political or social criticism ran the risk of drawing the communist label, and numerous authors, artists, actors, and intellectuals (both confirmed communists and people who were just labeled as such for their beliefs) were *blacklisted*, investigated by the Federal Bureau of Investigation (FBI), and banned from employment.

A Communist Cuba

t first Castro staunchly denied American accusations that he was a communist. He admitted that his brother Raul, one of the most important leaders in the revolutionary movement, was a communist, and that other members of the revn the United States, communism has a bad name and is associated with brutality, poverty, and "evil" regimes. The basic idea of communism, however, was to develop a society where everyone was equal. All land, property, and wealth would be held in common. Everyone would contribute to the community according to their abilities, and everyone would partake in the fruits of the community's work according to their needs. In this system, no one in the society would become fabulously rich, but nobody would be terribly poor either. The communist system was especially attractive to people who had spent years under the domination of others.

olutionary forces were communists. But Castro claimed that he and the revolution were neither communist nor *capitalist*, but *humanist*. He was not concerned, he said, with such labels, but with the quality of people's lives. Then, just a few months after coming to power, Fidel Castro did something that convinced many, both in Cuba and in the United States, that communist influences were far too strong in the new Cuban government. He began a nationalization program—a program where privately owned land and businesses were taken as public property to be overseen by the government.

The first things to be nationalized were most farms over one thousand acres. Farms of this size were mostly owned by wealthy individuals and big businesses (many of them sharecroppers: those who work someone else's land and receive a prearranged share of the crop's value less any charges.

agricultural cooperatives: farms that are worked by a group of people, sometimes for the purpose of providing food for the state.

defected: left one's country in favor of another.

sanctions: actions or penalties made by one country against another to force the other country into obedience.

American). Castro redistributed some of the land to the poor peasants and *sharecroppers* who farmed it and turned the rest into *agricultural cooperatives*. Enraged cattle ranchers and plantation owners began sabotaging crops. Anti-Castro rebellions broke out. Many feared the nationalization process would spread to every sector of the economy (and eventually it did). American companies employed more than 150,000 workers in Cuba, and these people feared losing their jobs if the Cuban government seized their workplaces.

The movement of Cubans to the United States swelled. These immigrants were not only Cubans who had supported Batista and feared Castro's reprisal, but also upper- and middle-class business people (many of them American educated) who feared losing their jobs, livelihood, or freedoms to a communist regime.

Over the next year, tensions grew between the United States and Cuba. Some of Castro's former allies, convinced that the communist influence was becoming too strong, turned against him and *defected* to the United States. Cubans in Florida began running air raids, first dropping anti-communist and anti-Castro leaflets over Havana, and later dropping bombs over sugarcane fields to destroy the crops on which most of Cuba's economy depended.

The United States was Cuba's biggest trading partner and purchased almost all of Cuba's sugar. Now Castro feared economic *sanctions* and perhaps even a military invasion. As relations with the United States soured and the prospect of a collapse in the sugar market grew, Castro signed a trade deal with the Soviet Union, ensuring that the Soviet Union would both purchase sugar and provide Cuba with needed goods and equipment.

Harvesting sugarcane

"Fidel Castro is not a communist now, but United States policies will make him one within two years."
—Soviet Premier Nikita Khrushchev, 1960

The Bay of Pigs

In response to increasing diplomatic relations between Cuba and the Soviet Union, increasing bombings by Cuban exiles in Florida, the mysterious explosion and sinking of a French ship in Havana's port (Castro blamed the United States), the passage of U.S. economic sanctions against Cuba, and rumors of a pending CIA-organized invasion, relations between the United States and Cuba finally spun out of control. On January 3, 1961, almost exactly two years after Castro's rise to power, the United States cut off all diplomatic relations with Cuba. On April 17, a CIA-organized invasion force, with the approval of President John F. Kennedy, landed on Cuban shores at the Bay of Pigs.

Not only had the United States been training the Cuban exiles who made up the approximately 1,400-man force, they had also been smuggling arms to the anti-Castro rebel groups popping up in Cuba. The CIA expected that once a U.S.-sponsored invasion landed on Cuban soil, a popular uprising would ensue and quickly depose Castro.

The CIA was mistaken. Castro may not have been popular among most upper- and middle-class Cubans, but he was more popular than ever among the majority of the population, whose life had improved since Castro's rise to power. Not only was there no popular uprising, Cuba's military was more than prepared to fight. After three days of heavy fighting, the invasion force was surrounded. No American forces appeared to assist them, and over one hundred members of the invasion force died in combat. The rest were captured and arrested. They were later released to the United States in exchange for goods like medical

*While international tensions mounted, school children
in Cuba profited from Castro's education reform.*

supplies and farm equipment, things that were now difficult for Cuba to obtain because of the U.S. *embargo*. The Bay of Pigs invasion was a disaster for President Kennedy and a huge success for Castro.

Both sides dug in their trenches after the Bay of Pigs. Castro responded to the United States by officially embracing communism, declaring Cuba a communist state, outlawing all political parties except the Communist Party, arresting thousands of people suspected of being against his government, solidifying relations with the Soviet Union, and *censoring* the media. The United States responded to Cuba by beginning plans for another invasion, hiring thousands of Cuban exiles in the CIA's anti-Castro programs, training assassins to kill Castro, bombarding Cuban airwaves with anti-Castro *propaganda*, and insisting that other nations join in the embargo against the island. Each country was completely unwilling to negotiate with the other, and before long, their hatred would bring the world to the brink of nuclear war.

"Naive art" by Cuban artist

The Cuban Missile Crisis

Although communism was expanding rapidly in the Eastern Hemisphere, Cuba was the first communist country in the Western Hemisphere. The Soviet Union was thrilled to have a communist ally so close to America's shores. The United States had already installed nuclear-armed missiles in Turkey, a country that shared a border with the Soviet Union. Now, the Soviet leader Nikita Khrushchev saw an opportunity to even the playing field. He offered to build missile bases on Cuba. Decades later in a PBS documentary, Castro would claim he didn't really want the missiles but was afraid of endangering his relationship with his only remaining ally and felt he couldn't refuse. Whether or not this is true, Castro did accept Khrushchev's offer, and construction of the missile sites began. Soon, nuclear-armed missiles would be poised within ninety miles of Florida.

When spy planes detected the missile sites, the U.S. government reacted strongly, and plans for an American military invasion of Cuba went into full swing. In Cuba, the army and the citizens prepared to resist such an invasion. American officials were once again surprised by the strength and enthusiasm of Cuban resistance. Intelligence sources advised President Kennedy that U.S. casualties would be high—perhaps thousands in just the first few days. If at any point nuclear weapons entered the equation, the results would be beyond anything the world had ever experienced.

Without consulting Castro, President Kennedy and Nikita Khrushchev struck a deal to have the weapons removed. Castro was furious that he'd been left out of the negotiations, but he also realized there was nothing he could do. The missiles were packed up and shipped home, and neither side would ever escalate tensions to such a dangerous level again.

In the aftermath of what became known as the "Cuban Missile Crisis," Cuba's economy took a nosedive. Not only had the country lost almost all its trading partners, it also lost almost all its well-trained, experienced professionals, intellectuals, and business people, the very people who help keep economies and governments running smoothly. In terms of basic needs like education, health care, housing, and access to a minimum amount of food, most Cubans have been better off since the revolution than they were before. Many people, however, felt that Cuba was a place where they could only achieve the minimum, the basics of survival, but never get ahead.

This loss of economic opportunity coupled with the loss of political freedom is what drove most Cubans to America's shores. Over the next decade, *defection* to the United States increased. The American government was happy to receive the exiles, who they saw as proof that communism wasn't working. Castro was happy to be rid of people who didn't support the revolution. By 1969, ten years after Castro's rule began, 400,000 Cubans had come to the United States, many of them on direct "Freedom Flights" from Havana to Miami.

Habla Español

crisis (cree-sees): crisis

rebelde (ray-bale-day): rebel

igualidad (ee-gwahl-ee-dod): equality

Luis Rodríguez, Llegada de mi Padre de Angola, *1997*

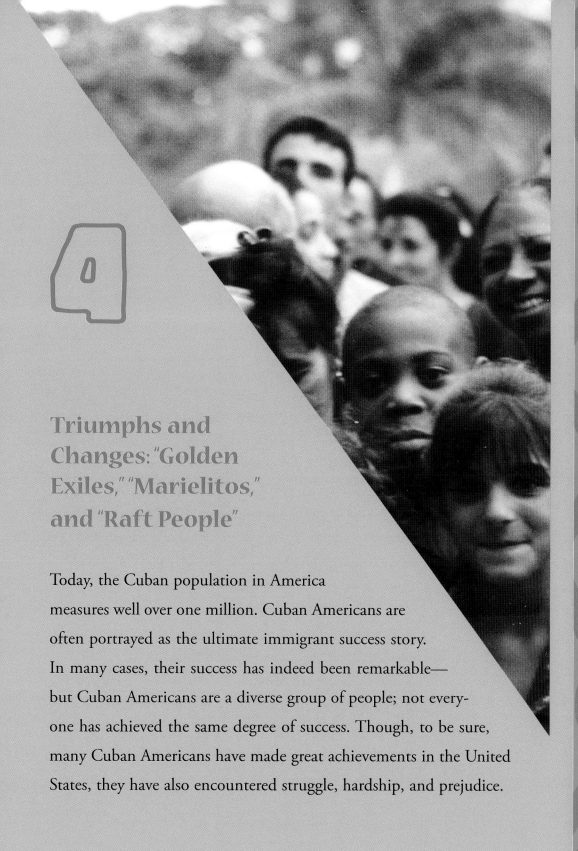

Triumphs and Changes: "Golden Exiles," "Marielitos," and "Raft People"

Today, the Cuban population in America measures well over one million. Cuban Americans are often portrayed as the ultimate immigrant success story. In many cases, their success has indeed been remarkable— but Cuban Americans are a diverse group of people; not everyone has achieved the same degree of success. Though, to be sure, many Cuban Americans have made great achievements in the United States, they have also encountered struggle, hardship, and prejudice.

Furthermore, not all Cuban Americans had the same experience on entering the United States. Some were welcomed, others were shunned. Some found ample support and help from the already established Cuban American community. Others found themselves locked out of that community. Their reception into the already established Cuban American community depended on when they came.

The Golden Exiles

In America, the new immigrants became known as the "Golden Exiles" for the wealth, education, and professional achievement that characterized them before their migration. Some had even been educated in America and spoke English well. The vast majority was white, saving them from much of the racism and discrimination that many people encountered in America. (Although many immigrants did encounter anti-Cuban sentiment.)

These social, cultural, and economic privileges made the Cuban community different from any immigrant community the United States had seen before. Many immigrants are forced to the United States by poverty in their homeland and come from rural backgrounds. In contrast, many of the Golden Exiles were urban professionals forced to the United States because their wealth and capitalist beliefs put them at odds with the Castro regime. Most of the Golden Exiles were also well-acquainted with American culture, knowledge that eased their transition into the United States.

A Cuban artist's portrayal of a young woman

None of this is to say that rebuilding their lives in the United States was easy for the new exiles. They were forced to leave everything behind and start anew in a strange land with a different language. But on arrival, they also entered a strong community (often of family, friends, and acquaintances from back home) that was ready to ease their transition, provide emotional and often financial support, and help make job connections. The Cuban immigrants also received an unprecedented amount of government services and access to programs that helped them secure loans, start their own businesses, and earn certification for certain jobs. In just a decade, they were a remarkable success story, having a higher family income than the American national average.

By 1970, the Golden Exiles lived in close-knit communities that dotted the U.S. map. Most of the exile community, however, continued settling in Florida, often right where they landed, in the southern city of Miami. Soon Miami was a cultural *enclave* for the exile community. Once in Miami, these immigrants set about rebuilding the lives they had left behind. As they did so, they re-created many of the places

émigrés: people forced
to leave a country for
political reasons.

they had loved in Cuba. Restaurants, streets, parks, coffee shops, and stores all bear the names of similar places back on the island. Today, some people call Miami "Little Havana." Walking through certain sections of this teeming city, a person could almost convince himself that he is indeed back in Cuba.

The Marielitos

By the early 1970s, the flow of Cubans into America had slowed dramatically. Castro realized that the loss of so many talented people had significantly harmed the country, so he stopped the Freedom Flights in 1973. The American government had also put more restrictive laws in place to stem the flood of immigrants. Although hundreds of thousands of Cubans had entered the United States during the 1960s, only tens of thousands came in the 1970s. Then, in 1980, a new flood of Cuban immigrants inundated Florida's beaches in what became known as the "Mariel Boatlift."

The catalyst for the new rush of émigrés seemed to be Castro's 1978 decision to allow Cuban Americans to make one-week visits to their families back on the island, some of whom they hadn't seen in twenty years. The response was tremendous as relatives poured home. But something else also poured into Cuba along with the long-lost families and friends—American consumer goods. The visitors brought all kinds of things, from food and useful household appliances to luxury items like designer clothing and televisions. The Cuban people suddenly saw in bright, shiny, brand-name detail the luxuries available in

A Cuban festival

uring the Great Migration of Golden Exiles, the U.S. government expended a huge effort encouraging Cubans to settle anywhere other than Florida. Approximately 16.4 percent of the Cuban American community settled in New York, 12.7 percent in New Jersey, 9.1 percent in California, and 3.6 percent in Illinois. Smaller Cuban American communities also formed in Colorado, Minnesota, Texas, Missouri, and many other states. Forty-five percent, however, remained in Florida, and after a number of years, the majority of those who settled elsewhere returned to the southern state where so many of their friends and family members lived.

67

More consumer goods are available in the United States than in Cuba.

America. For many it was an awakening, a revelation of what they lacked in an economically depressed socialist state. A sudden surge of people wanted a chance at life in the land from which these amazing things had come.

Once again, Castro responded to the unrest with an *If they want to go, let them go* attitude. In April 1980, he declared that the Peruvian embassy was open to receive emigrants. More than eleven thousand people packed their bags before the week was even up! When the response was so large, Castro decided he would allow emigrants to go directly to the United States (instead of having to pass first through Peru) by boat out of Mariel, one of Cuba's port cities. The result was amazing. The moment Cuban Americans in Florida got word, many went to their family boats (mostly pleasure boats for tooling around Florida's coastal waters, not for ocean voyages) and set sail for Cuba. In Mariel, thousands mobbed the docks, waiting for friends, family, or anyone who would give them a ride.

But before long, the Mariel Boatlift turned sour. Some of the fishing boats and other private boats that pitched in to help began charging the "Marielitos" exorbitant sums for the trip. They also stuffed people into small cabins, overloading the boats and pretty much guaranteeing that, should the boat go down, everyone would drown. Some people even died of suffocation during the trip. Castro also got into this spirit of *opportunism*, using the boatlift as a chance to rid himself of hardened criminals and people with mental illness whose care was very costly to the state.

Unlike the political exiles of a decade earlier, the newest Cuban arrivals were not welcomed with open arms. For one thing, the American media dubbed all Marielitos criminals and mental patients, even though only a few hundred of the thousands who immigrated fit this description. There were other prejudices as well. The earlier exiles had been Cuba's economic elite and Castro's biggest critics. Not only were they valuable to the American economy, they were valuable to the American government. The new arrivals were just regular working-class people looking for a better life, and few Americans were happy to see them looking for that life on their shores, shores that in the 1970s were facing significant economic difficulties of their own.

Then there was racial prejudice. Like America, Cuba had a long history of discrimination against black people, so before Castro's revolution, the people who achieved higher education, gainful employment, and upward social mobility in Cuba were almost exclusively white. The vast majority of the Golden Exiles (some statistics say as many as 98 percent) were white, but more

opportunism: the practice of taking advantage of opportunities as they are presented.

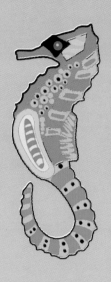

Some Cubans are descended from African slaves.

stigma: a mark of shame.

Many Cubans face prejudice in the United States.

than 40 percent of the Marielitos were black. They found themselves discriminated against, not only by prejudiced Americans, but also by many of their own countrymen.

To make things still worse, many of the Marielitos arrived without the proper immigration documents. Those who couldn't obtain refugee status or couldn't find sponsors (people who agreed to take financial responsibility for the new immigrant) were locked in detention centers. Thousands languished in legal limbo. In the end, many spent over a decade in what was essentially a prison, only to be returned to Cuba.

After four months of boatlifts, approximately 125,000 Cubans had flooded into America—approximately 1,042 people each day!—and America and Cuba were both ready to close the gates. The rush to leave his country (nearly one million people had filed emigration documents) was hugely embarrassing for Castro. It was also deeply disturbing for the U.S. government, which worried about the effect the new immigrants would have on employment rates, housing, crime, and social services. In October of that year, Castro called an end to the emigration, and the United States breathed a sigh of relief.

Despite everyone's fears, however, within ten years, the vast majority of Marielitos had proven themselves to be just as capable and industrious as the first Cuban Americans. For many, however, prejudice was difficult to overcome. *Stigma* is still attached to the Marielito name.

The Raft People

n 1990, the Soviet Union collapsed. All over the world, people celebrated the one-time superpower's downfall—but in Cuba, the world-changing event threatened to be a death-blow to the already-struggling economy. Cuba had now lost one of its last (and certainly its most important) trading partners. Fidel Castro declared the time a "special period" and asked all Cubans to conserve and sacrifice to see the republic through this hard time. Soon, however, many Cubans felt desperate—desperate enough to face the shark-infested Florida Straits, clinging to nothing more than flimsy rafts and homemade boats.

Radio Martí

n May 20, 1985, the first broadcast of Radio Martí could be heard in Cuba. Part of Voice of America, an official service of the U.S. government, Radio Martí was named for the late Cuban writer and activist José Martí. The network broadcasts news about Cuba and Cubans—to Cuba. These are stories that those living under the censorship of Fidel Castro can't hear in ordinary radio broadcasts. Messages from family members in the United States are also sent back via the broadcasts.

Some Cubans were willing to risk death to go to Florida.

People escaping Cuba in homemade rafts was nothing new; it had been happening from nearly the beginning of Castro's rise to power. What was new was the number of attempts suddenly being made. Most people realized that though Florida was close in relative terms, ninety miles of ocean water was no small feat for a homemade craft with only paddle-power and almost zero navigation ability. Even if you made it past the guns and military ships that patrolled Cuba's shores, you were very likely doomed if you weren't rescued by a passing fishing boat or Coast Guard vessel. Death from thirst, sunstroke, drowning, and shark attack awaited those who risked the sea.

But now there were thousands of people willing to take those risks. In just four years, the number of Cuban "raft people" rescued from Florida's waters increased from 466 in 1990 to 4,169 in 1993. In 1994, when Castro announced that the police and military would no longer hinder ocean departures, a mass exodus reminiscent of the Mariel Boatlift's early days ensued. In just over a month, more than 30,000 Cubans took to their rafts and boats.

Most of these newest émigrés were rescued by the U.S. Coast Guard. Unfortunately in some cases, only their empty vessels or remains of destroyed rafts were found. Once aboard the Coast Guard's ships, however, the Cubans were not guaranteed entry to the United States. Instead, most of them were taken to the U.S. military base at Guantánamo

Bay and never achieved entry to the United States. The U.S. government then instituted what has often been called the "wet feet versus dry feet" policy. If Cuban refugees made it to U.S. soil and had relatives in the United States, they would be released to those relatives. If the refugees were picked up at sea, however, and could not prove they needed *political asylum*, they would be immediately returned to Cuba. The flow of desperate Cubans willing to risk the ocean waters never stopped, but in the face of new U.S. policy, it did slow considerably.

political asylum:
safety granted due to
danger caused by one's
political beliefs.

ow you know about many of the historical conditions that pushed Cubans toward American shores and the journeys many took to get here. No matter when they came or how they got here, once in America, Cubans set about creating something new: the Cuban American community. Next we'll take a look at some of the ways Cuban Americans have kept their culture alive and contributed to America's cultural mosaic.

⊞abla ⊟spañol

viaje (vee-ah-hay): journey

inmigrante (een-mee-gron-tay): immigrant

refugiado (ray-foo-hee-ah-doh): refugee

Not all Cubans wanted to leave their homeland.

73

Luis Rodríguez, El Tres Viejo, *1997*

5

Ties to the Past, Eyes on the Present: Cuban American Culture Today

Carlos could see his mother was uncomfortable. Bringing her to the office party had been a stupid idea. He had thought it would give her a chance to see where he worked, meet his colleagues, and begin understanding what the last twenty-five years of his life had been like here in America. Now he wondered what he had been thinking. His mother seemed self-conscious and overwhelmed. She kept tugging at her clothes—new purchases Carlos had insisted on getting for her even though she'd been appalled at the cost—and although she spoke English well, she kept asking Carlos to translate everything into Spanish.

75

Life is less materialistic in Cuba than the United States.
These Cuban boys have made toys out of wooden pallets.

Picking his mother up at the airport two days ago, Carlos had been shocked to see how much time had changed her. She was far from the energetic woman he remembered. When he was young, she had always seemed so strong, and she practically ran everywhere she went. Now she seemed small. Wrinkles worked deep creases into her face, and she walked slowly and carefully.

When Carlos had decided to make the journey to America, his mother had refused to come with him. All these years, she had insisted she never regretted the decision. Perhaps that was why Carlos felt so desperate to prove that life in America had been good to him. This was the first time his mother had visited, and Carlos wanted her to know that he'd made the right decision coming here.

Over the last two days, Carlos had taken his mother to see many things—the mall filled with all kinds of stores and gadgets she'd never seen before, the grocery store with its astonishing bounty, the rows upon rows of shiny new cars at the Ford dealership. Carlos thought these things would impress his mother, but instead she made other observations, like how large his house was (she said it felt like everyone would get lost), how independent his children seemed, and how much garbage the household generated. Now, driving home from the office party, she observed another aspect of Carlos's life in America—that all his coworkers called him Carl.

"Hijo," his mother said in that scolding tone Carlos remembered so well, "you've become *Americano*."

Carlos turned to his mother and smiled sheepishly. "Don't worry," he tried to assure her. "You just got here, and we haven't seen each other in a long time. But in a few days you'll see that I'm still your Carlos. In all the important ways, I'm still Cuban."

*Did you know...
The turtle is a symbol for good luck in Cuban culture.*

Carlos's mother is clearly concerned about what has happened to her son in America. His American lifestyle makes her think he has forgotten his culture—that he is now more American than he is Cuban. Carlos assures his mother this is not the case. He believes the changes in his life are surface changes and that deep down he is still culturally Cuban.

Carlos's mother's fears are common ones felt by many people throughout the United States and the world. Parents often feel anxious when they see their children speaking English better than they speak Spanish or adopting values that are different from the ones their elders hold. Tension between gen-

Older Cuban Americans may have difficulty adjusting to the American lifestyle.

77

erations is common to all human beings, but it can be especially evident and perplexing to immigrant communities, who have already lost their homeland and now fear losing their children and culture as well.

In chapter 1, we described culture as a glue that needs to be refreshed if it's going to maintain the stickiness that holds communities together. Fortunately, Cuban American families have many opportunities for cultural renewal. Though America has certainly brought changes to their lives, Cuban Americans have a proud cultural heritage, and cultural memory usually begins in the home.

Family

Cuban Americans generally have small families in the sense that, on average, parents have only one or two children. In fact, Cuban American women have one of the lowest total fertility rates (the total number of children a woman will give birth to in her life) in the United States. Nevertheless, many Cuban American households can seem like they are teeming with people and activity. This is because Cuban American families are often close-knit, with grandparents, parents, aunts, uncles, sons, daughters, and cousins all living close together and gathering frequently.

The tendency toward close-knit families goes back to the way life was in Cuba. In Cuba, extended families almost always live together in small houses or apartments with multiple generations under one roof. Furthermore, the neighborhood becomes

A mother and daughter attending a Cuban church service

an extension of the family. Friends and neighbors are always visiting and dropping by. Cuban Americans of the older generations might complain that life in America is too impersonal. Americans value big houses, privacy, independence, and individuality—not the first values that come to mind in Cuban American households. In many ways, Cuban society is more open. American families often live far apart, and some individuals tend to care more about themselves than about each other. Of course, over the generations, many Cuban American families have adopted more of an "American" lifestyle. To say all Cuban American families live close together or gather often would be an inaccurate *stereotype*, but significant numbers of families continue to prefer living in close communities.

Cuban American families also blend many *progressive* ideals with *conservative* values. For example, in the average Cuban American family, both parents work. This is considered a progressive social value (whereas desiring that women work only in

In the past, the quince symbolized a girl's entrance into womanhood. Today, the quince has taken on additional meaning, especially in the United States. Crime, drugs, gangs, teen pregnancy, and other social difficulties are prevalent in some parts of America. In areas facing these problems, the quince has become a celebration of "making it" through these dangers and reaching womanhood safe, alive, and (parents hope) virtuous.

the home is a conservative social value). Cuban American women achieve just as much education as their male counterparts and value professional employment.

At the same time, many families place equal value on marriage, maintain traditional or conservative attitudes toward dating, and hope their children will marry within the Cuban American community. But as in all cultures, children often have their own ideas about things like dating and marriage, and many young people choose marriage partners from other cultural backgrounds.

The Quince

Cultural traditions are also part of many Cuban American families. One good example of a family-oriented Cuban cultural tradition is the quince. A quince celebrates a girl's fifteenth birthday, the day she is believed to emerge from childhood and enter adulthood; it is sometimes compared to a debutante ball. On this special day, the girl dresses in a beautiful gown (conventionally, the gown was pink, but today it may be white or any pastel color) and is attended by up to fourteen female and fourteen male friends. The big day begins with an intimate church service in which only family and close friends take part. There is usually a special portion of the service in which the priest speaks to the girl about what it means to be a woman. After the church service, the quince crowd swells as the girl's other guests arrive for a dinner followed by a dance. Here, the girl and her fourteen attendants might perform a very complicated dance called a *contradanza*. It's also traditional for the whole crowd to participate in a slower-paced dance called *el danzón*. Today, pop music is also a regular feature of a quince celebration.

Quinces can be small affairs or huge parties, depending on how much money a family can afford to spend on their daughter's big day. For many Cuban girls, it's a day they look forward to and plan for weeks, months, or even years beforehand. The quince is much more than just a birthday party. It symbolizes a permanent change in a young woman's life. From this point on, she will no longer be considered a child; she will be a woman.

In years past, the quince celebrated the preservation of the girl's virginity and announced her readiness for marriage. Some families even considered the quince more important than their daughter's wedding. Today, the quince can mean different things for different people, but the emphasis on a transition from girlhood to womanhood remains the same.

Religion usually plays a central role in the quince celebration. (Remember, the day begins with a church service.) For many Cuban Americans, religion is another way in which their culture is honored, expressed, and renewed.

A window in a Cuban church

Religion

eligion plays a key role in many people's cultural lives. Most Cuban Americans are either Roman Catholic or Protestant, both Christian religions. Christian religions are based on the belief that the Jewish teacher, Jesus of Nazareth, was the son of God. According to Christianity, Jesus was sent to earth to bridge the gap between God and humanity, so human beings could once again reside with God in heaven.

Roman Catholicism, one of the oldest forms of Christianity, was the religion of the Spanish Empire. Brought to Cuba by missionaries, it became the leading religion on the island. Protestantism, on the other hand, was the form of Christianity most commonly practiced in the United States, and as American influences increased on the island, so too did conversion to Protestantism. Cubans also converted to Protestantism once they immigrated to the United States, sometimes because of their specific religious beliefs, but often because they thought it would help them gain acceptance in their new land.

Another commonly practiced religion among Cuban Americans is Santeria, a religion that developed on the island but has many of its roots in African religions. Many people describe Santeria as a polytheistic religion (meaning that it believes in the existence of many gods). This is somewhat misleading. Santeros (people who practice Santeria) believe that there is one all-powerful god called Olodumare or Olorun. In this way, it is similar to monotheistic religions (which believe there is only one god). What causes the confusion, however, is that Santeros also believe there are many lesser spirits called Orishas (some might uth Behar is one the most provocative and important artists and scholars working in America today. Her Jewish-Cuban American heritage has been an important influence in her work, giving her a complex perspective on what it means to be a member of a cultural community. Behar's family moved to Cuba from Europe. Behar was born in Havana, but she moved with her family to New York when she was still a child. She became an anthropologist after earning a Ph.D. from Princeton University, and focused much of her study on Spanish, Mexican, and Cuban history and cultures. In 1988, just a few years after beginning her anthropological work, she won a highly prestigious MacArthur Foundation "Genius" Award. Since then, she has achieved many more accomplishments and awards and is now a writer, poet, and filmmaker in addition to being an anthropologist. Two of her most famous books are *Translated Woman: Crossing the Border with Esperanza's Story* and *The Vulnerable Observer: Anthropology That Breaks Your Heart.*

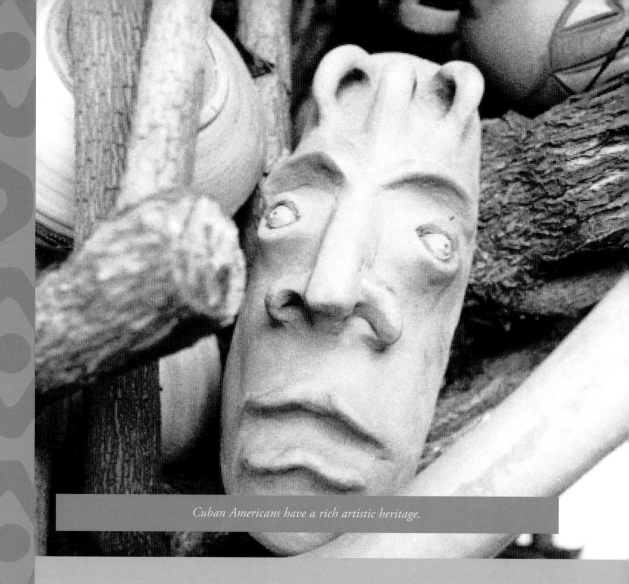

Cuban Americans have a rich artistic heritage.

call them gods), who interact with people as Olorun's emissaries. People pray to these spirits and enact rituals that focus on them.

The Santerian belief system is actually quite similar to Catholicism in the sense that Catholics believe people called saints can intercede with God on behalf of living people. In fact, Santeria incorporates some elements of Catholicism, and historically, Santeros used the Catholic saints as a disguise for their Orishas, since being discovered practicing Santeria could lead to serious punishment. There are even Cuban and Cuban American Catholics who have adopted some Santerian practices, and many Santeros describe themselves as devout Catholics. Common elements of Santerian rituals include drumming, dancing, spirit possession, and sometimes animal sacrifice.

Although they are often overlooked, a significant number of Cuban Americans are Jewish. In the 1920s, Cuba's Jewish population numbered around five thousand. Most Jewish people came to Cuba fleeing persecution in Europe, and later many moved to the United States when Castro came to power.

The Arts

The arts are also vibrant parts of Cuban American culture. Throughout the traumatic exile experience, the arts have been a way for Cuban Americans to remain connected to their island and to each other. They've also provided a much-needed outlet for many of the painful and conflicting emotions that have accompanied the exile or immigrant experience.

Cuban Americans have a rich literary tradition that stretches back to José Martí and beyond. Today's generation of Cuban American writers are often just as concerned with themes of exile, freedom, and independence as their predecessors were. Some important contemporary Cuban American writers include Pulitzer Prize-winning novelist Oscar Hijuelos, poet and scholarly writer Gustavo Pérez Firmat, Pulitzer Prize-winning playwright Nilo Cruz, best-selling novelist Christina Garcia, and award-winning novelist Achy Obejas.

Cuban Americans also use the visual arts to explore their experiences, record their culture, and deal with the confusion and upheaval that was once so common in their lives. From murals gracing walls in Miami to paintings hanging in New York City's Museum of Modern Art, Cuban American art contributes to

Eleggua, the chief Orisha

Another Orisha, Yemaya

85

oday, Cuban Americans teach in some of America's most prestigious colleges and universities. Antonio Benítez Rojo, one of Cuba's most famous writers, came to the United States in 1980. He has taught at Harvard, Yale, Brown, and other respected universities. Today, he teaches at Amherst College in Amherst, Massachusetts. *Sea of Lentils, A View from the Mangrove,* and *The Repeating Island* are some of his most famous works. Gustavo Pérez Firmat, another important Cuban American writer, was born in Havana, Cuba and raised in Miami, Florida. In 1995, he was named Duke University Scholar/Teacher of the Year for his exceptional contributions to that school. Today, he teaches at Columbia University in New York City. Dr. Manuel Justiz came to the United States when he was twelve years old. As an adult, he studied political science. He later taught education at the University of South Carolina and then became the director of the National Institute of Education. In 1990, he changed careers again, becoming the Dean of the University of Texas at Austin's College of Education. There he has helped rebuild the school, which is now ranked in the national top ten.

Nilo Cruz, playwright

America's entire cultural landscape. Some important Cuban American artists included photographer Ramón Guerrero, photographer/artist Maria Martínez-Cañas, artist and cartoonist Enrique Riverón, and artists Arturo and Demi Rodriguez.

From classical musicians like pianists Horacio Gutiérrez and Jorge Bolet and classical dancers like ballet star Fenando Bujones to popular artists like salsa legend Celia Cruz and pop diva Gloria Estefan, music and dance are also essential components of Cuban American artistic life. Music and dance popular on the island have become mainstays of Cuban American entertainment in particular and American entertainment in general. Salsa, an energetic type of music and dance that incorporates traditional African rhythms with other musical styles like jazz and rock-and-roll, is immensely popular. Even today's youth are experiencing a resurgence of interest in learning traditional Cuban dances, dances their grandparents did back on the island. Furthermore, many Americans regularly enjoy Cuban-inspired music without realizing they have the Cuban American community to thank for the pleasure.

Achy Obejas, Cuban novelist

ther arts also continue to nurture the Cuban American community. Although tobacco is generally a controversial subject in America, Cuban cigars have long been an icon of Cuban culture, and the art of cigar rolling is still well respected among Cuban Americans. Although the famous Cuban cigars can't be imported to the United States, high-quality cigars rolled by Cuban artisans are made in the United States.

Enrique Riveron

uban American attitudes and practices toward the family, religion, and the arts are just some of the ways that the Cuban American culture keeps ties with the past as it is renewed in the present. Individual Cuban Americans have also made important contributions both to their communities and to America as a whole. We'll take a look now at the lives of just a few of these amazing individuals.

Habla Español

hijo (ee-hoe): son
familia (fah-mee-lee-ah): family
religion (ray-lee-hee-own): religion

arte (ahr-tay): art
música (moo-see-cah): music
bailar (bah-ee-lahr): to dance

Luis Rodríguez, El Entierro, *1997*

Making America:
Cuban Americans Who
Have Touched Our Lives

The people of Cuba have a long heritage of creativity and innovation. Immigrants to America brought with them this rich legacy. Their talents have enriched the American artistic scene, and their industry has broadened the scope of U.S. businesses. You may be surprised how many household names are Cuban Americans!

Desi Arnaz

Desi Arnaz

esi Arnaz was one of the first Cuban Americans to gain national recognition in the United States. Born in Cuba in 1917, he moved to the United States as a child. As an adult living in Miami, Florida, he worked as a musician and performer, making his living drumming Cuban-style rhythms. In fact, he is often given sole credit for bringing the conga, a Cuba dance of African origin, to America.

Arnaz's real chance for fame came, however, through his American wife: the popular actress and comedian Lucille Ball. In 1951, CBS studios wanted to create a television show based on Ball's unique style of comedy. Ball refused, however, to do the show if Arnaz was not permitted to play her husband. At first, the television studio did not want to give in. Lucille Ball was supposed to play an "all-American" girl, and they would not cast the Cuban Arnaz as her "all-American" husband. CBS was convinced that American viewers would not find a Cuban husband believable in an American television show. But Lucille Ball wouldn't give in either; Desi Arnaz *was* her husband, so she wouldn't participate unless he was permitted to play this role on TV. CBS eventually relented, and *I Love Lucy* was born.

machismo: exaggerated manliness often characterized by aggression.

I Love Lucy became one of the most successful programs in television history, and Arnaz's character, Ricky Ricardo, was an important part of the formula. His culture, however, was rarely portrayed in a flattering light. Ricky Ricardo's character was riddled with stereotypes of Cuban manhood. Ricardo was full of *machismo* and was variously portrayed as a crooning "Latin lover" or as a hot-head bursting with his "Latin temper." The show routinely poked fun at Ricardo's "Cuban-ness" and incorrect use of the English language. At the same time, however, Arnaz was one of the first Cuban performers to achieve national fame in the United States; in a time when Spanish-language programming was nonexistent, Arnaz's Spanish-speaking character was, if stereotyped, still groundbreaking.

Celia Cruz

Long-popular throughout the Americas and gaining popularity throughout the world, salsa is an energetic type of music that sets feet tapping. For decades, Celia Cruz was salsa's biggest star. In fact, Celia Cruz was one of salsa's creators, meshing varied musical styles from jazz and rock-and-roll to traditional Afro-Caribbean rhythms to create a new sound.

Though the exact date is disputed, Celia Cruz was born in Havana, Cuba, in the 1920s. As a child, she was a skinny little girl with a really big voice. Celia was one of many children, and her family struggled financially. There was no money for music lessons, but Cruz had other opportunities to display her talents. She traveled around Cuba, singing in contests and sometimes winning. Success in the music business, however, was by no means guaranteed. In fact, it was pretty unlikely. In Cuba, professional music was men's realm, and many doubted whether a woman could sing the rhythms, attract fans, or sell records.

In 1950, Cruz proved everyone wrong (including her father who was not particularly supportive of her singing career). At the time, she was singing with the band La Sonora Matancera, and they had just released a record. Not even all the band members were sure that having a female vocalist was a good idea, but the record was a success, both in Central America and in the United States. Celia Cruz and La Sonora Matancera became national favorites of the Cuban music scene. In 1960, however, Cruz and the popular band decided to leave the country where they had so much success and come to the United States.

Celia Cruz

When Cruz arrived on American soil, she suffered setbacks in her career. Not until the birth of salsa and Cruz's adoption of it as her signature style did she regain widespread popularity. (Although based largely on Cuban musical styles, salsa was born in the United States.) Cruz became famous, not only for her distinctive and powerful voice, but also for her flashy style, colorful costumes, and ability to electrify an audience. Decade after decade, her popularity and importance grew until she was both an icon in the Cuban community and a legend in American music. By the time of her death in 2003, she had recorded twenty gold albums and more than fifty albums in all. Today, Celia Cruz lives on, both in her music and in the generations of young performers she inspired.

Roberto C. Goizueta

oberto C. Goizueta was born in Cuba in 1931. His father was a wealthy sugar producer who gave young Goizueta a privileged place in Cuban society. A member of the wealthy elite, he was able to come to the United States to attend Yale University, where he graduated in 1953. With a degree in chemical engineering, Goizueta returned to Cuba.

As a member of Cuba's most powerful classes, Goizueta could have easily started out at the top. He could have entered his father's business and one day taken over the reins, but the young Goizueta didn't want to step into his father's shoes; he wanted to start out on his own and prove his abilities. Instead of stepping to the helm of an already powerful business, he answered a newspaper ad for a job in Coca-Cola's Cuban outlet in Havana.

At first things went well for Goizueta. He had a good job, was happily married, and had three children. But after Castro came to power, Goizueta's position with an American company was not secure. The family made an agonizing decision. They would send their three children ahead to Florida, and they would soon follow, leaving everything they'd worked for behind. On the day Goizueta followed his children to America, he had $40 in his pocket and one hundred shares of Coca-Cola stock to his name.

In the United States, Goizueta continued to work for the Coca-Cola Company, and each year he moved a little further up the corporate ladder. Soon, he was one of the highest-ranking Hispanic people in the American business world. In fact, by 1981 he had achieved the highest position possible within the Coca-Cola Company: chairman and CEO (chief executive officer).

Things, however, were not always easy at the top. Coca-Cola was (and is) one of America's largest companies and is known around the globe as a symbol both of the American business world and of America as a whole. Many people both within and outside of the company resented having a Cuban at the helm of such an American icon. But Roberto C. Goizueta *epitomized* the American dream: he arrived as an immigrant with almost nothing and, through determination and hard work, became one of American business's greatest success stories. Who better to run one of America's biggest companies? Furthermore, Goizueta was a brilliant businessman, and soon the numbers spoke for themselves. During his sixteen years as head of Coca-Cola, the business's stock value rose from four billion dollars to $145 billion.

Roberto C. Goizueta's accomplishments went well beyond his business savvy. He also believed deeply in helping others rise above difficult circumstances to achieve success. He gave numerous lectures and speeches on topics such as citizenship, corporate responsibility, and personal achievement; donated money to universities; and committed himself personally and financially to *humanitarian* causes. He won numerous awards for this work, including the Herbert Hoover Humanitarian Award (1984), the Olympic Order Award

> "My story boils down to the uniquely American idea that a young immigrant could come to this country with nothing but a good education and a job as a chemist, and thirty years later have the opportunity to lead one of the world's best-known enterprises."
> —Roberto C. Goizueta

Gloria Estefan

*epitomized: served as
the ideal example.*

*humanitarian: a
person promoting
human welfare and
social reform.*

(1988), the NAACP Equal Justice Award (1991), and several honorary doctorates. Roberto C. Goizueta died in 1997.

Gloria Estefan

loria Estefan has achieved incredible fame and fortune in America, but she is no stranger to hardship. Born in Havana, Cuba, in 1957, Gloria's family fled Castro when she was little more than a baby. Gloria's father wasn't present for much of her early childhood. While Gloria was still a toddler, he returned to Cuba in the Bay of Pigs inva-

"You never know what
life has in store for
you, but I believe there
are certain things one
is meant to go
through."
—Gloria Estefan

sion. Gloria and her mother were living in a poor area of Miami at the time, and during his eighteen-month incarceration in Cuba, they struggled and worried over his fate.

Gloria's father was returned to the family, but hardship too would return. Her father later fought in the Vietnam War, where he was poisoned by a chemical called Agent Orange that was used to kill Vietnam's dense foliage, exposing enemy troops hiding within. Gloria's father survived the war, but his health was never the same. He developed multiple sclerosis, a debilitating disease of the nervous system that can eventually cause paralysis. Back home, he was unable to work, and Gloria cared for him while her mother supported the family.

These were difficult years in Gloria's life, but music helped her get through the trying times. Uncomfortable with her weight, glasses, looks, and shyness, she spent much of her time alone in her room with only her guitar for company. She passed long hours teaching herself the tunes she heard on the radio. In her community, people recognized that Gloria had talent, but proba-bly no one, especially Gloria herself, ever dreamed she would one day be an international star.

The beginnings of Gloria's musical career were similarly hum-ble. While attending a wedding, Gloria's mother coaxed her to sing a few songs with the band. The band's keyboardist, Emilio Estefan, was impressed. The one thing the Miami Latin Boys needed, he thought, was a strong lead singer. Gloria began mak-ing weekend appearances with the band. Soon they adopted a new name: the Miami Sound Machine. The band began releasing albums, first in Spanish and then in English, and soon became the first band to rise simultaneously to the top of both Spanish and English music charts.

Gloria quickly became known as much for her dancing and gutsy performances as for her voice. Gloria and Emilio wed and

Not all Cuban artists and musicians are famous.

Musicians performing in a Cuban café

had a son. The Miami Sound Machine seemed unstoppable as it took a ten-year run on the music charts. Then, in 1990, hardship and tragedy revisited Gloria. A semi-truck crashed into her tour bus. Gloria's back was broken, and her prognosis for a full recovery was poor. Not only was the dance diva unable to perform, she might never walk again.

Just as she had done in her teenage years, Gloria turned to music for solace and inspiration. Within a year, she made what many people thought to be a miraculous physical recovery. She and her husband had a daughter and she was also back on the charts with her poignant album *Into the Light*. The song "Coming Out of the Dark" clearly communicated her struggle to emerge from tragedy into triumph. It hit number one.

Today, Gloria Estefan continues to entertain and inspire millions. She has released sixteen albums, of which five went gold, three went platinum, two went double platinum, three went triple platinum, and one went quadruple platinum. Ms. Estefan dedicates much of her time not only to her music career but also to serving others through charitable causes.

Habla Español

azucar (ah-soo-cahr): sugar

tragedia (trah-hay-dee-ah): tragedy

triunfo (tree-oon-foh): triumph

milagroso (mee-lah-grow-so): miraculous

Luis Rodríguez, Noche Buena, *1997*

7

What Does
the Future Hold?

The waves crashed over the inner tube, threatening to loosen the little boy's grip. His salt-caked hair fell into his eyes, making them sting. He looked out over the water; nothing but grey for as far as he could see. He was so thirsty, hot, and hungry. He concentrated on keeping his eyes open. There were sharks out here, and if he fell into the water. . . . He couldn't think about that. He was all alone in the endless ocean, but he was too stunned and frightened to cry.

n Thanksgiving day, 1999, a little Cuban boy named Elian Gonzalez was found floating in the waters off the coast of Florida. The boat he and thirteen other travelers had been crowded on sank into the churning Florida Straits. Ten members of the party, including Elian's mother, drowned. But five-year-old Elian clung to his inner tube and survived.

In the months after Elian's rescue, controversy in the Cuban American community (and in America as a whole) reached a fevered pitch not seen for years. Usually when the Coast Guard rescued Cubans from the ocean, they took them straight back to Cuba. Elian's situation was different. Here was a traumatized child whose mother had died and who had narrowly escaped death himself. Furthermore, he had family in Florida. Now they were mourning the loss of Elian's mother and were desperate to take the little boy into their home. They said they wanted to give him a better life in America than he could have in Cuba. So Elian was taken to his relatives' home, but soon his story grew more complicated.

It turned out that Elian's father was still alive; in fact, he hadn't been on the ill-fated boat at all. He was back in Cuba, frantic to learn what had happened to his son. He described how he'd arrived home from work one day to find his son gone, kidnapped by his mother and taken to America. Now, Elian's father wanted him back, and soon some of America's most powerful lawyers and government officials were involved in the boy's case. The little boy also became an unsuspecting poster child for a renewed anti-Castro campaign. He was just five years old, but international politics was warring over his fate.

After drawn-out court battles that achieved much international attention, it was decided that Elian's place was with his father. Elian's relatives, however, were unwilling to give the little boy up and see him returned to Cuba. As the dramatic events unfolded, federal agents stormed the home and seized Elian. The court battle, however, continued all the way to the U.S. Supreme Court. The Court made its decision, and Elian returned with his father to Cuba.

Elian Gonzalez

105

idealized: gave something or someone the characteristics of one's standard of perfection.

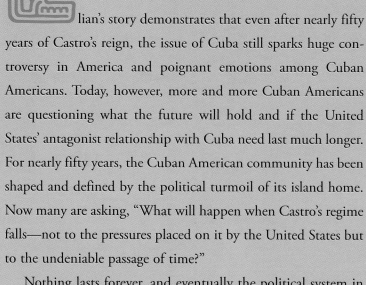

lian's story demonstrates that even after nearly fifty years of Castro's reign, the issue of Cuba still sparks huge controversy in America and poignant emotions among Cuban Americans. Today, however, more and more Cuban Americans are questioning what the future will hold and if the United States' antagonist relationship with Cuba need last much longer. For nearly fifty years, the Cuban American community has been shaped and defined by the political turmoil of its island home. Now many are asking, "What will happen when Castro's regime falls—not to the pressures placed on it by the United States but to the undeniable passage of time?"

Nothing lasts forever, and eventually the political system in Cuba will change. Castro will die, and a new leader will come to power. When this happens, many other changes in Cuba could follow, and Cubans Americans will have to make decisions. Will those who still consider themselves "temporary" exiles return to the land of their culture and birth—or will they stay in America where many have now lived most of their lives? If they do return to Cuba, will they find that the "Cuba of yesterday" for which they have longed was really a myth, an *idealized* picture they developed during their years of exile? Will they find the land has irreparably changed and no longer feels like home? Or might they find they are the ones who have been irreparably changed and no longer feel at home in their native land?

Although their relationship to the island remains strong, many Cuban Americans today feel that after years of exile, they are no longer completely Cuban. Now they are also American, undeniably part of America's cultural mosaic. When changes do come to Cuba, Cuban Americans will face them as they have

Cuban graffiti

faced so many other changes in their lives: head on, ready to keep Cuban culture alive, in all its forms.

abla spañol

cambio (cahm-bee-oh): a change

cultura (cool-too-rah): culture

mosaico (mo-sah-ee-coh): mosaic

Timeline

October 12, 1492—Christopher Columbus lands in the Caribbean Islands.

1511—Hatuey and his people flee Hispañola for Cuba and the
    first Cuban revolution begins.

1861–1865—The American Civil War takes place.

1863—President Abraham Lincoln abolishes slavery in the United States.

1868—The Ten Years War begins in Cuba.

1886—Spain abolishes slavery in Cuba.

1895—Revolutionary José Martí, Father of Cuban Independence, killed in battle.

1898—U.S. battleship Maine explodes in Cuban harbor; United States blames Cuba.

1902—United States declares Cuba an independent nation.

1933—United States helps overthrow President Gerardo Machado; Fulgencio Batista
    becomes Chief of the Military.

1940—Cuba holds first free elections, and Fulgencio Batista is elected president.

July 26, 1953—Fidel Castro begins his drive to overthrow the Cuban government.

January 1, 1959—President Batista and his closest allies flee to the Dominican
    Republic; Castro and his supporters assume leadership.

January 3, 1961—United States cuts off diplomatic relations with Cuba.

April 17, 1961—America launches the Bay of Pigs invasion.

October 1962—Cuban Missile Crisis involving the United States, Cuba,
    and the Soviet Union.

April 15–October 31, 1980—The Mariel Boatlift brings a new flood of Cuban immi-
    grants to Florida.

May 20, 1985—Radio Martí, part of Voice of America, begins broadcasting in Cuba.

Thanksgiving, 1999—Elian Gonzalez rescued off the U.S. coast.

Further Reading

Conde, Yvonne M. *Operation Pedro Pan: The Untold Exodus of 14,048 Cuban Children*. New York: Routledge, 1999.

Cramer, Mark. *Countries of the World: Cuba*. Milwaukee, Wis.: Gareth Stevens Publishing, 2000.

Creen, Linette. *A Taste of Cuba: Recipes from the Cuban-American Community*. New York: Penguin Books, 1994.

Eire, Carlos. *Waiting for Snow in Havana: Confessions of a Cuban Boy*. New York: The Free Press, 2003.

Fernández, Alfredo A. *Adrift: The Cuban Raft People*. Houston, Tex.: Arte Público Press, 2000.

Gay, Kathlyn. *Leaving Cuba: From Operation Pedro Pan to Elian*. Brookfield, Conn.: Twenty-First Century Books, 2000.

Grillo, Evelio. *Black Cuban, Black American: A Memoir*. Houston, Tex.: Arte Público Press, 2000.

Hoobler, Dorothy, and Thomas Hoobler. *The Cuban American Family Album*. New York: Oxford University Press, 1996.

Olson, James S., and Judith E. Olson. *Cuban Americans: From Trauma to Triumph*. New York: Twayne Publishers, 1995.

Zinn, Howard. *A People's History of the United States*. New York: HarperCollins Publishers, 2003.

For More Information

Afro-Cuban Web
www.afrocubaweb.com

Castro Speech Database
www.lanic.utexas.edu/la/cb/cuba/castro.html

Cubamigo: Bilingual Web site about life in
Cuba today: www.cubamigo.com

Cuba 1997: A Web site about the 14th
World Youth and Student Festival
www.firspage.org/cuba/

Cuban American Alliance
www.cubamer.org

Cuban American Heritage Festival
www.cubanfest.com

Cuban American National Council, Inc.
www.cnc.org

The Cuban American National Foundation
www.canf.org

The Cuban-American Softball League
www.caslsoftball.org

Cuban Exile Newspapers at the
University of Miami
www.uflib.ufl.edu/flnews/cuban.html

Cuban Research Institute
lacc.fiu.edu/centers_institutes/
?body=centers_cri&rightbody=centers_cri

The Elian Gonzalez Story
www.as.miami.edu/las/Elian/elianmain.htm

Exploring the Culture of Little Havana:
A Learning Community Project
www.education.miami.edu/ep/LittleHavana

Facts about Cuba from the CIA's The World
Factbook
www.cia.gov/cia/publications/factbook/geos/cu.html

Institute for Cuban and Cuban-American Studies
www.miami.edu/iccas

Publisher's note:

The Web sites listed on this page were active at the time of publication. The publisher is not responsible for
Web sites that have changed their addresses or discontinued operation since the date of publication. The publisher will review the Web sites and update the list upon each reprint.

Index

Biographies

Autumn Libal is a freelance author and illustrator living in Vancouver, British Columbia. She received her degree from Smith College and has written numerous educational books and articles for children. Other Mason Crest series Autumn has contributed to include NORTH AMERICAN FOLKLORE; PSYCHIATRIC DISORDERS: DRUGS AND PSYCHOLOGY FOR THE MIND AND BODY; NORTH AMERICAN INDIANS TODAY; YOUTH WITH SPECIAL NEEDS; and WOMEN'S ISSUES: GLOBAL TRENDS.

Dr. José E. Limón is professor of Mexican-American Studies at the University of Texas at Austin where he has taught for twenty-five years. He has authored over forty articles and three books on Latino cultural studies and history. He lectures widely to academic audiences, civic groups, and K–12 educators.

Picture Credits